Configurations

Configurations

Trevor Code

Ódrerir
Melbourne 2012

Ódrerir: the Muse's Cauldron.
41 Jackson Way, Dromana, Vic 3936, Australia

©Trevor Code, Dromana. 2011-2012
This book is copyright. Apart from any fair dealing for the purposes of study and research, criticism, review, or as otherwise permitted under the Copyright Act, no part may be reproduced by any process without written permission. Inquiries should be made to the publisher.

The poems in this volume were written in 2010-2011, and were edited and revised where necessary in 2012.
"Tin Shed in the Rain," "Intertextuality," "Through an Open Door," "The Papers," "Strata," and "Too Many Universes" were included in *Lightstream*, ed. Brian Edwards, Mattoid/Grange, Deakin University. 2011.

Cover photograph and design by the author, with very welcome assistance and advice from Sylvie Blair of Bookpod.
The cover image is the ancient town wall of Wexford Town, County Wexford, Ireland. This wall was partly destroyed by Cromwell's forces in 1649.

©Black and White Photograph of Trevor Code by Tricia Veale
©Black and white photograph of Trevor Code by J.Hillersten
Editor: Jane Hillersten.
Published by Ódrerir Books
41 Jackson Way, Dromana, Vic 3936, Australia.

In Old Norse literature and mythology, Ódrerir was the muse's mead, and also the cauldron in which it was brewed.

Printed by Bookpod, Australia.
www.bookpod.com.au

ISBN: 978-0-9806725-4-1

Author's Note:

A major scholar has recently pointed out the tendency, fuelled by Creative Writing courses, for an assumption that literary works, of any time period past or present, are inescapably autobiographical. After all, it is easier to gossip about the author's, or composer's, or painter's sex-life and deprivation than the work itself. As a poet, I am not writing autobiography. I don't think Shakespeare, Whitman or Dickinson were doing so either. And I don't find it particularly helpful to reduce the arts to "self-expression". I engage in an art which may be speculative, imaginative, philosophical, probing, subject to trains of thought, association of ideas – or even caprice. Like a mathematician, I grapple with symbols; unlike a mathematician I perceive, and sometimes play with, the inexact nature of the symbols or words which make up our language. Whitman said it was "a language experiment." I am not "I"; "I" is not I – or me. I place things on the page, objectively at times, but sometimes swept up in the emotions of the theme or the work. I hope that the reader might experience such emotion too – and hear it. I refer to the titles of two late volumes by Robert Lowell: *Notebook*, and *History*. They morphed into versions of the one book. I am engaged with the terrain and the climate, the daily events often of Dromana and the Mornington Peninsula in Victoria – but in my Irish poems I am heavily wrapped up in the traditions, history, ballads and fate mainly in Wexford. In *Which Way the Wind* (2010) I argued that the reader completes the line and the poem. The book belongs to the reader.

TREVOR CODE

This book is dedicated to Edward Codd (1834-1869)
to the heritage of his entire family
and to all of his descendants.

CONTENTS

A Tin Shed in the Rain	13
Intertextuality	14
Through an Open Door	15
My Mother's Death	16
The Papers	18
Strata	19
The Season	20
Remit	21
The Salvia	22
The Last war	23
The Voices Haunt Him	24
The Escape	25
Tok Tok	26
That Old Axe	27
Sorting	28
Whisht	29
Slow Cooking	30
Too Many Universes	31

In the Best Season	*32*
To the Victors the Spoil	*33*
Selskar Abbey	*34*
Tourist Precinct	*36*
All Things Much the Same	*38*
The Potato as Disquisition	*39*
The Circling of Tongues	*40*
The Descent	*41*
Popo	*42*
Of freedom	*43*
Sudden Squall	*44*
That Moment by the Fig Tree	*45*
We Send but They Return	*46*
Talking the Way	*47*
Over This Sea of Faces	*48*
Koalas in the Night	*51*
The Lost Sheep	*52*
Feeding	*53*
Still	*54*

Witness	*55*
Pleasure	*56*
Round the Oblong Table	*58*
On the Playful Banks	*59*
What Poetry Is	*60*
Shades	*61*
The Dancer	*62*
Meditation at a Crossroad	*63*
Portrait of a Passenger	*64*
Henry the Puppet	*65*
Tribal Rituals	*66*
Going and Coming	*67*
Hearing it Not on the Radio	*68*
The Song of the Fallen Soldier	*69*
We hear Their Voices	*70*
Old Prints	*72*
Vanished Years	*73*
The Gift of Roses	*74*
A Thousand Mirrors Cannot See Your Soul	*76*

I Would Give You	77
Distance	78
In this Autumn Light	79
World Travel	80
Coastal Vista	81
It's Held in Blood	82
The Granite Stairway	84
The Path of Blood	85
Our Lady's Lake: Wexford	86
Castletown Carne	87
The Old Ballad	88
Reading the Graves	89
Something of a Ballad	90
Exequy	91
The Emigrant Hero	92
For Drowned Crewmen	93
History Repeats	94
Emigrant Ancestor	95
A Question or Two	96

Dreaming on my Land	97
The Barquentine	98
The Wexford Three	99
Of the Croppy	100
Three Sailors	102
Lament	103
A Sectarian Struggle	104
Poets of the Ascendancy	105
Ballad of Crusades and Chastity	106
Aftermath	107
In the Whiskey Bar	108
We Travel On	109
The Band on Parade	110
As Time Works its Way	111
Sin	112
Old Coat on a Peg	113
The System	114
Voices in the Bar	115
You Will Wait Here	116

Stay a Little	*118*
The Flood	*119*
Museum Town	*120*
The Dolls	*121*
The Worm	*122*
Stitches	*123*
Don't Take Your Bat to Town	*124*
Waiting for Father	*125*
That Almost Perfect Poem	*126*
Crossing on the Ferry	*127*
In Some Future Time	*130*
They Seemed to Bloom	*132*
I Was Not There	*133*

A TIN SHED IN THE RAIN

Behind the locked tin doors, the boxes –
some covered in coated fabric –
stand on the concrete floor where I think
the sludgy rain escaping from the pipe
will run down deep and make them rot.

But that is how it is: in an absent thought,
the door unlocked, I find at last
the gutter which I scooped has done its work
and the seepage of sand and mud was slight.

There is no smell, and even the spiders
vanquished by poison, have left no thread,
nor that appalling stink they leave behind
where they hunt and breed all night.

But I need a cloth to mop the drops
where heavy rain has forced its way –
and a tape to close the ancient leaks
before I wrestle with bark, leaves, sticks
and blocked downpipes which choke and dry.

INTERTEXTUALITY

It is many years since I have seen a flea.
Indeed, I have seen that very dangerous thing
a tick, much more recently than a flea –
and I know the ravages conveyed by bites
and embedding: disease, fever, plague.
I muse a little on John Donne's "The Flea,"
which through a mixture of bodily fluids
seems a playful permit to concupiscence.
Well as a dwarfish thief proclaimed at night
blood will have blood – of course it will.
But there was a song, for a baritone in glee
which had the mirthful refrain, ha-ha! a flea!
a comedy of itching in the scratchy courts
while we might sing and scatter in a deeper voice
and laugh to tease or scrape a funny bone.
Once I knew a fat and slobby man, quite great
in bulk and talent, who taught a motley crew
of players and I was one of them it seems.
I sought to parody my master with his strut
with flip-flops, pout, and belly sticking out.
He'd muse and puff, a-gargling in his throat –
And he was a scholar then to snort and quote:
Big fleas have little fleas upon their backs to bite them
and little fleas have lesser fleas and so ad infinitum.
Well so the nursery's wisdom seems to make my song
But great things born of little prove it wrong.

THROUGH AN OPEN DOOR

Whenever I open a door
I do not know what comes speeding through
sometimes on magpie's wings
and what that other brings:
this mulch of words and fractious designs
imprints on suggested cornices
prizes that strangers have won
or might have said they've won
in another jurisdiction –
all this with a foot in the door.
The teasing hordes come noisy up the road
shouting and whistling as they wave
papers directions arbitration
and the long curl of many personal triumphs
back to a teased out history
not ephemeral I know
but neither in this aiding of my peace
or making anything secure at either end;
and then the beating heart as I feel it
knowing in this the edges of my brain
my personal shell of skull
and in my chest the ribs
things that I feel at heart
and as I close my eyes I feel the throb:
aorta aorta aorta as they say.

MY MOTHER'S DEATH

Whenever I think of my mother's death
I think of a train

which is a strange thought because though she travelled
by train
I do not recall going with her

not in those later years
but we lived not far from the station

and she said, unlike those other people
she would prepare for age and death, wisely

run classes on retirement, make friends
talk on the telephone, have tea and biscuits.

The train whistles and the crossing signals
could be heard from our house.

We could see the train pass by to the station.
What we did not understand was the schedule

that the train was unstable and noisy
yet it was relentless as the timetables by which they
depart.
[...]

It made a mockery of her mind:
it is not yet, but it's most unfair, she said

I thought I would have more time
but anyway, I'll know when it's time to go.

THE PAPERS

Each Tuesday we empty the bins
or baskets, into the large plastic wheelies
and every second week recycle
papers, bottles, tins, and card boxes;
I trundle out armfuls of news
and programs, political comment, cartoons
and what is tired when a few days old.
I talk to the lass at the bookstore,
a friend, and I think she understands
her trade, that the presses all must churn
to bind up paper which will sell a moment
turn yellow or curl and then be tossed.
How many pages do you think
will we look at next year, or after that
promoted by prizes, flushed with campaigns
and the moment of bustled excitement?
When it's over it's over, it glowed
for a moment, was caught in the chatter
obeyed all the forms and the formula
the edges of titillation, prospect of death.
And we talked – but a lady, who once
so she told us, had worked in a bookstore
was asking, most sweetly, and do you?
she said, well, do you have Shakespeare
apart from school texts, say *As You Like It?*
well no, I'd not think so – no demand as they say!

STRATA

He woke, to a deadly sky
cold feet, the wet
and the way the damp warmth percolates
creating horizontal strata of seeming air –
he remembered archaeology: the dig
but can the climate be this thing?
the vase was broken, but the stopper
all the bottles, some green, stamped
of a time beneath the rubble of the place
speculation that this was infamy
pieces of broken pottery told an age
the dark streets hid their secrets
but in this town, its inner crannies
the way the paths were used, the cries;
as the residents age they must transform
and write long passages in scrolls
slowly thinking of how to hang
history, or testimony, to witness
corrosion and the way each regulation
was political, not as a law
but as a regimen so firm
that no one rebelled, no one it seemed
could break the past, nor water it down
but what was known by all of them and said
with a finger poised outside the mouth.

THE SEASON

We have stowed the winter clothes in boxes
having no room, and the yet the air
is cooling still, as if all things on hold.

Australia Day, they say, is where the summer ends
at least the holiday, the kids all back to school
perhaps to swelter in the late arrival of the sun

A soggy day, cool air that seeps through vents
and round the country rivers burst and seep
through levies, or cascade throughout the town

We are cut off, they say, from what is ours;
the locals know the clever ways are rotten
the mud is flowing past verandas, into floors

and up, at times to windows and to roofs.
They show it on the television news, alarm
appeal, escape, and how the cost will rise.

We sit at a frozen desk, and glimpse the sun
tomorrow comes, they say, and is another day
at last the flood recedes, the heat will come,

something will open, dry out tracks of stuff.
They talk of climate change, and wonder what:
next day, next month, and what might lie ahead.

REMIT

live awhile
to tell the story
absent from bliss
not so acute
caught in things
as witness to
a sort of danger
on this hill
or plateau
the vagaries of men
and women too
do as they do
at times without
a plan or thought
but sharp it is
as a serpent's tooth
so some would say
but really cut
and sealed in blood.

THE SALVIA

The salvia in all their varieties
and the fuchsia – bursting blooming imports!

when the breezes and gentle sun entice
and acrobatics of bird life – a gesture of goodwill

we might celebrate if not assailed
late at night hear distances

out of focus, carried to us
the night has this quality – of amplification.

We look to the reports of weather
what will come is always what will come.

certain though they be – predictions
bunch us together in expectation

a calm bright day with flower petals
is no assurance – the picture is static:

the wind and the relentless sky are constant
and harmony can be maintained.

THE LAST WAR
Did you ever think this war would end wars? Eric Bogle

For all the dead in peace, many I think
died of what the sentimental call
a broken heart, not of the verminous stress
that living creates when families survive
in a way, by counting coin and gain.

It is the brother or sister who forsakes us
but then, these twins of ours, not kin
but somehow simulacra, made for show
and hustle, how they sought to mount
by various sorts of climb, to leap or lie.

How could you kill a friend by telephone?
Now if you say, that's just the way things fall
then I agree, it is they fall that way
and we must place some wisdom on the slate
replace despondency or sultry turns of hate
with knowing, and with prophecy it seems:
that humans are this kind, and do like that.

THE VOICES HAUNT HIM

The voices come back to haunt him
    murderer   slaughterman   traitor

It was the good that you opposed and killed
now we pay taxes and we have lost much

How can he look back on that?

> *You marched for freedom, sang your chorus*
> *Exchanged your family for the forces.*

They will grieve that you do not weep
they feel the tears inside their sleep.

Oh, you'd defend him, listen well.
He's wounded and his heart's in hell.

You cannot tell this tale again
it has been told, we don't know when.

Their children wear medals, with discordant bands
they play old music no one understands.

THE ESCAPE

I am not hearing you fearing you
steering you, or being steered by you
fierce and unrelenting thing, you sprite
where the guttered street is catching
and we might rip to cross, and mind
traffic through here is unrelenting, crude
the path runs down to the sea, the road
winds down away to the swirling tide
and another town, where nothing can be told
but the same yarns of capture and escape:
lies we tell ourselves and still believe.

TOK TOK

When the multiple birds cry out
not in an ecstasy of song
but in alarm and conflict
we notice how their cries of combat
open spaces for punctuation
of the other who just watches this
and seems to say Ahem! Ahem!

THAT OLD AXE

with that old axe you should wear gloves
remembering that the skill is not the heft
but partly in the balance and the swing:
most of the eye, so you step back
afterwards, in some satisfaction:
you did this way what many could not do
and took it with you in a kind of sling –
walking requires a similar sense of self
so the step is balanced and in time
but now the eye is turned another way –
the balance which is always far and keen
links great horizons to the mark within.

SORTING

we empty them out on the table
rattle or stir them with our fingers:
the colours are so predictable, primary
and in a way we know they are the same –

then we begin the wasteful inspection
taking them one by one for scrutiny
hoping that among their manufactured shapes
there will be one thing, notable, different

and we can say to each other with satisfaction
we have found at last that special thing:
we did not believe it was that, but we hoped
a mark, a scratch, some indentation –

now we shuffle the rest to their box
and as we treasure that one, something fades:
we think, but this one, which we chose
it now appears so tame, just like the rest.

WHISHT

whisht rabbit
and the little cooking bird
or long whistle
in decorum
after all the storm
has passed
we find it evocative
of others such
and we do not remember
the diary
and its pent papers
when we fell
there were items
whistling and popping
but never quite
affording words

SLOW COOKING

In a slow oven, the daube
and marinade, the beef
carrots tomatoes olives, and the herbs

Is it that we should eat this
or be embalmed by its wafting smell
the hours of ancient cooking?

Not finesse, not artful cuisine
but the flourish of a time we had
before all things were chopped and sliced.

Time, I will say, is seasoning
how we recall the way this day
is bound with flavours, and is firm.

Old pastures, and the tales of gallantry
the ladies in the tower, heraldic theme.
I look at them and shudder at the dream.

TOO MANY UNIVERSES

too many universes are locked in
primly upon themselves
like poems going nowhere
resplendent in their sticky words
besmirched upon a page
they are, in their sense, apposite
fine as a tray of fruit
their blemishes exposed
their balances prim
and so the satellites keep whirling
the moons appear to swim
and by this contemplation
we think the telescopes are not too large
for distances so dreary
the gods may see them as a doily
or marker of some journey
but we forsaken
sit and nod – crosslegged
and let them lead us
essentially nowhere:
and yet they circumambulate
in their slow disintegrating spin.

IN THE BEST SEASON

In the best season the crops grow green
they light up the moistened soil
and the farm tools are cleaned for fresh toil
it's the look on the weathered faces must be seen.

They have but little but there is some hope
even in the crumbled stones of my old tower
where perched ancient birds who watched the sower
and saw the way men pulled the box and rope.

This is an ancient craft, like when they temper
the blades or tines for tilling and slaughter
the plaiting and knotting each new crafted halter
the tying down of beast or men that whimper.

I watch from well above, as if almighty
but I am past, I gave what arm could give
slaughtered an evil thing so you could live
and now you pay my toll to nine and eighty.

There's blood let into ground, and rest for iron
the battles fade to old men's tales of youth
what heroes said, and what they did in truth
and how they feasted, filled with heat and wine.

Now you must dream and settle down to doze
but I, I'm facing chambers drear and void
my feet still echo and I cry aloud –
bring back the clamour and my noisy foes.

TO THE VICTORS THE SPOILS

To the victors the spoils and dismembering
heads on pikes or entrails in the fire
a fox's carcass on a fence, and even for luck
a scruffy rabbit's foot, before the myxo plague.

All of these mounds mark famous victories
we move by death from one step to another
and history proclaims our sense of destiny
the poet talks of murdering a brother.

And once the path is set to go this way
I cannot see the backward turning
some clerk of books will say with a wise nod
you'll see, it's just the way it is, though odd.

We do these things, because it's what we do
and even looking back, we see no place
where any other path was carved and held
and blood was not the craft we used.

SELSKAR ABBEY

I

The red scarred bricks are the balustraded walls.
The towers point to the heavens, and this
old Catholic abbey and fallen Church of Ireland
a profession of late faith. It is a monument to hope
and failure, to the loss of love, the dereliction
of our lives. We are saddened by it and old bricks.
The roof is down. What can we say?
The lost love in the convent led to agony:
the abbey was destroyed by Henry's men,
and desecrated once again by Cromwell.
So what remained? not fortress but a relic,
built for love and one kind of human faith.
My love is dead and I surrender to the Lord.
But my love lives and I am bound by oath.
The windows and the roof are gone – bells taken
to Liverpool. What is this church which tries
to bridge hostility, and sinks in its own ruin?
The gates are locked, and it is not safe to see.
I will come back as an old man, summon graves
call vanquished men again to speak to me!

II

This is a mere shell of a church, blue sky for a roof
and its bells, where are its bells, sounding
if they may sound, in a faraway port across the sea
where emigrants embarked as they fled the deadly
famine?
We built walls of rocks and iron, fires of religion
our perished love and our grieving here were lost
in their stone sadness. In this place we demolished
faith, and yet rebuilt, old as old, these monuments.
Here Henry Two came once, to claim a realm
in imperial repentance, for his friend dismembered
and the other Henry, a Tudor, failed royal stud,
killer of women, said tear all down, no candle lights.
The church is derelict: no people and no tax;
the bushes reach skyward through the rooftop gap.

TOURIST PRECINCT

By the old castle wall with its worn stones
a plastic trash bin on wheels stands still –
on the other side an official notice.
The towers like rooks in a chess set
are stained in our imagination by blood
of past generations, and broken implements
of war, farm tools turned to use
as battle irons, where the rebels died
when chains of family history were lost
and the march was slow as we trudged
into or away from town – our dereliction.

Today the tower has new steps inside
and guiding leaflets, well-edited and printed
to tell the tourist that this ground is old
somehow older for the scars and the dead fields
and the docks from which the lost departed
to tell their stories in an emigrant land
after fierce dark journeys on the sea
sold it for a song or two, they'd say
and when the maps are drawn, this line
will mark the border where they came
and where as traitors they were forced to go
always, as they said, to westwards
to hear a language lost from birth.
[...]

In silence, and the vacant fields like desert
where we await the call of bell or knock
and then the sudden change, and we say, is it?
the visitors who come are taking stock.
how paltry to be thus and count the beans
the papers and the quarrel taken off the track
the way the frames are set so you don't ask
or how a staff now leans as it was left
so what is hidden is concealed as lore
a thankless task that's buried at this time.

ALL THINGS MUCH THE SAME

My journeys have been safe enough
and comfortable enough if these things are
though tiring, and we arrive in a temporary blast
discovering only that all things are the same
or much the same, the pavement cracks
the illusions of old towers, the voices in the street
the sense of misdirection, but finding home
as easily as one of the folding board games
and a dice to throw for the movement of counters
the constructed hazards, the loops and setbacks
where chance is a glimpse of a pony or a beautiful dame
and the rows of coffee shops have similar signs
there must be rickety tables and chairs
smoke drifting where permitted, away from the voice –
we arrive, and we stop, and we are still:
hurtling planning dreaming through this time's cascade
into a morrow of imagined terrors and errors
from which we must have escaped as you see
or we could not tell it, and we laugh at our folly
pledging to tell it one day over afternoon tea
or a banquet, in the random gathering of hearers
and we say, how can this be, that they came
when you think of it, as close as they did?
We are called, called again, and we try to dispel
the edges of ghosts and the ones who are peeping
like the children who were, as they hid, at the door.

THE POTATO AS DISQUISITION

The potato is it? or rather the poisonous blight
the desolate rot which shakes the land, black
and to eat what must exude a foul smell
boiled down to make a kind of evil stew
and the heart cannot stand it, some there die
of hunger, but others, weak of contamination
curse as they lie shivering, and are saved
broken, survive in the damp, and they know
they must now leave, find work and haven
where it's bright, there's riches to be had
in the chance, and the music you can play
to remember as it was, this was a land
once gave blessing, and a feast be had
before this thing, known as a putrid curse
and its ooze, as the blood that is sucked
and the wealth that is taken of beast and grain
by red-faced assertive possessors of the land.
Then come to me, my lovely, and I would tell you:
but there's no waiting that can cure it
the letters you write home will find a way.

THE CIRCLING OF TONGUES

You cannot say the tongue is lost
the language speaks itself in winter trees
and the sea-burst lake where we have walked
the language in the rock, and in the bird
which circles to us, then in time away
the language hears itself within our hearts
and tells of gladness and the way we blend
the way we sing to ourselves and then repeat
phrases not sung but felt within the breath
and telling deeds as stories not of fate
but how the love and valour folded here
and rocked with us in times that are not old
but wheeling as that bird which comes again
the tongues they say the tongue, the edge of throat
the syllable of throat the coughing night
where some are hungry and yet yearn to sit
or where they thirst and wait for us to bring
the chosen bounty of our toil and loud it is
the way that we as kin will always know
the whispered sounds of words we thought were hid
but never lost, if robbed, if captured here
and then like water touching with its lip
the shore where foam has settled as it will.

THE DESCENT

I have to come through it, as I descend
in declining circles, like a wonderful kite
or some black bird which curves its path
with never a flicker of its rigid wings

why should we think like this, the hefty climb
the visionary descent, and the way the rumbling trees
prop up at last as they were a sign before
and rolled across our landscape like a card

we see with binocular vision what was hid
but we retain no debt to it at last
the distant figure, not to scrape
the wondrous scratchy foliage, or the scent

or the hidden trails of tiny rigid things
which left their mark, but never stayed in sight.

POPO

In his essential clownish posture
the adventure of his adventure
and his foolish caper
magician-like, he strides
in a forlorn cap
and makes the maidens blush .

OF FREEDOM

In the bleak sun of this season in the wind
I see advertisements flashing on my screen
and never staying still, distractions as they show
in a slave state, where we glimpse democracy
in the way that stunts are worked, this world awry.

I see the people coming in their hundreds to the halls
and voting as they must, for only one good choice
the cipher man or woman with a poster face
who will take away their dreams and hopes
but tell them how he cares and lays the ground
and they'll believe him, and they'll shuffle on.

It will be a starved time, the dread invasion
from the tropic north, from the other cities
the invasion of the redneck men who come
demanding freedom as they should, to claw
to take this future and to turn it to a profit
for a day at last, to grasp what things they can.

I am not the whipped slave, I am no longer black
I no longer work the harvest, I sit and rock
old birds go squawking, cut down trees
take away the medicines which might ease the pain.
Oh then, we call it, dreamtime of our freedom.
They say we want this thing, its future now.

SUDDEN SQUALL

the little pellets of hail
bounce at my feet
and I hunch
as I hustle
to shelter
on a slimy
blowy day
when the rattle of hail
and bustle of elements
distract me from the dream
of the sunny morning
through which we came.

THAT MOMENT BY THE FIG TREE

That moment by the pear tree
or was it fig?
We could not tell in its winter grey
and we were too sodden to speculate
but we thought of details that mattered
the pruned cut perhaps, not made yet
the yellow jacket of the mailman
shedding this drenching rain
the contemplation of the way the path
becomes a drain, and all banks up.
We will wait for things to bud
in another more benevolent season
and we will shovel old stuff in the barrow
dig compost in and wait
to see what may return and grow
later, much later, when there's time to bask.

WE SEND BUT THEY RETURN

It's from the returning container ships we take
message and comfort: we send but they return.
This is a fable old as any tale
and there's little magic in it, just to touch.
They say it's commerce, and the dredged way
tracking the small blue world with crates of things
reciprocal perhaps, the balance and the game.
In this, fair judgement, or the strip of war
we'll cut the labels off and in a crop grown
along with all the artefacts of trade
we'll say, our champion made smart work of it
piled up their heroes' heads, and caught the bones –
conquest, is it? the way we give or take
survival, or the way the ocean flood
is yet our flow as well, our bonus here.
It's getting fired, close cut as you will find
bonanza, or what's promised, and the steel.
You need a temperament for chess perhaps
or stud games, or you spin the fragile wheel
but how it lights is nothing
to demonstrate the gull you bring to play:
to win, or then to take the winner's pay.
And generous, with a heavy face
to give a little gift to aid the help
and those whose aid is given to the world.

TALKING THE WAY

I'd have no one, and no way to go
the lines cut and recovery uncertain
under the earth they say, is surely safe
but where it fails, it's like old Humpty
in the rhyme, and no one knows the pieces
or how to gather them and fit them into place.
What does one do? We learn to wait
and so the battery's flat, tank empty
and all the power is off – there are books
or pages half completed, no one knows.
Silence is giving, and the strength of it
now echoes, I can note the clock
the whine of trees and distant rumble.
In a time you'd say like this
the land seems further from the sea
the town is separated from the highway
the market is a place where traders walk
and bags or baskets ache on a tired arm.
Whistle me some signal bird. I hear
the logic is forsaken, all the lines
cut off and ruled or bent to re-adjustment:
so negate the time of chatter and the will
to go on talking, in this old way or that.

OVER THIS SEA OF FACES

over this sea of faces
the grand hall inquisitorial
and the groups expectant of dismissal
or those who wait for something wise
should the speaker choke
or should he snuffle
bite a tear, and clear his throat
this is the age of discontent
after so many promises
so much advance
the way great engineering
turned to trivial commerce
and we found that all device
could not divide the benefit from toy
in this degeneration of the game
for passing yet again a slice of time
between the rising and the end
and toting up our satisfaction
then, you'd say, so what
it is the pleasure of our instruments
why did God give them
if there were a God
but for our use in any way
and haven't we advanced enough
we have advanced machines
so let them be set loose
[...]

to run design make music
guard our shores, and feed us
the proliferation of our slick ideas
the way our money halts
the way our shares still bob along
while we decide that cooking shows on ice
or sex on ice, or sport on ice
or life on ice, might mean our death
or even play at resurrection
in a campsite where a steely God
will wear a viking helmet
and a great bear fur
and stir a pot upon an open fire
returned from battle or the hunt.
Did you think that God and angels
all were tribal, spent their time
in war and retribution
carrying off the loot, the slaves
rewarding those who brought them gifts
themselves of course
and promised fealty
but everything they wrought
was simply neolithic
till the coming bronze
made sharper spears and swords
{...}

and blood was then as red
as any sun, and in our paint
and in our song, we told
of how the battle went
and how it goes again
like procreation, and fatality
shock then, the pallid faces turn
the clock is at the archway
and the maker says
the time it keeps runs backward
we must take
a new beginning
and a dream constructed
of the trees and how we climb
or coasts and how we forage
the strangers who are there
if we would see their craft
and how we wait
impassive for the end.
Go out from here and then from there
all systems may be built or broken
and the revolution has begun
it starts in clouds of dust
as false foundations start to yield
and we are left quite naked unrestored.

KOALAS IN THE NIGHT

The bears are roaring overhead
we say they're bears
the way that lovers talk
koalas then, who make the noise
the males we think who have this howl
it's mating time, and in the trees
they climb and rock
and do the things that lovers do
this springtime short of fancy
turns to love or what they say
high in the trees, or on the grass
the facts are known
and in our time we open up
the gates of all that humans know
not much and very short
but when we part
we know each other just that bit
and more perhaps than when we came.

THE LOST SHEEP

Who is seeking
for what
orientation
the disclosure
all the netted brambles
what we hear
might it be
just crows
and not bleating
what trades we make
fade or cross
and there is no
distance
under the blue
confusing sky

FEEDING

We are alone
the small grey birds hang
upside down as they suck flowers

And the cold wind blots the sun

We stare into a closed distance
dream of a dazzling sun
but the bone is chill

Oh we long for sweet
and we echo the shrill calls
assertive not alarmed

Say then I have come
I come in triumph here
and I take what I can

But we acknowledge loss
send out the post
and wait to hear

It was not the taste stirred us
nor the chance of serendipity
upside down.

STILL

Coming home again, in the same bed
I watch the ceiling light
and time or years are unreality
this is the time I woke so many times
to places and festivity and I recall
the dearest faces that are lost to me
the way I walked on beaten trails
unknown to my pale limitations
and the way I always hoped to meet
as I do now, someone
still known, still waiting
only lost because my dreams
did not fulfil the prospects of the day.

WITNESS

a piece of me
looking for it on the step
where the bank square is closed
or the brown flood lies
it seems a fragment curls
like skin on a pot
and is air light
unclaimed
I lift my eye
engage in scrutiny
returning to this place
for a dire encounter
incomplete
but the events
unwrap themselves
out of sequence
and so slowly
drop in place
with no image then
but white yarrow
which bobs in the air
bringing a small glow
pieces of its witching truth.

PLEASURE

Pleasure
      everlasting
black as day
      in a garden
seeing eternity
      on all sides
the solid
          pity
and Nature
      she rose in quiet
and hid her love
      with wine and virtue
the eyes and dreams
dying
      do not weep
sweet berries
      explain nothing
but music
         come back
with the sea mist
      breath   .

ROUND THE OBLONG TABLE

If you take the corners off it is still oblong
not a sharp rectangle, but hinting at the dream
of contour or the circle, the stately board
where heavy dishes pause and glimmer
and the conversation, after grace and introduction
is wise perhaps, profound, but never tedious
as if, we'd say, the guest said this
and we'll remember how enlightened in response
the repartee and tale or gently doctored praise.
So they would gather, move to the simple gate
and only choke or rev-up gently as they loosed the brake
gave decorous signals and a wave, and drove away.
The solid edges of that table set the tone
of all that is ceremony: and we mark it down.

ON THE PLAYFUL BANKS

In the shallow water – nets
the crabs slip under in their cheerful scurry
and here it is warm, the sand's heat
somehow magnified by the face
of an afternoon breeze
the children at play with their plastic toys
artificially bright as a hundred sweets
the silhouettes of dogs
and small children run along the bank
caught by the orange sky
in this, there is the peace of recreation
tired limbs cry out for balm
and there is always salt on the tongue.

WHAT POETRY IS

poetry is a small and dangerous art
always risky even when reaching for the sublime
or sudden recognition. He may be a poet
of both consistency and diversity
where the poems have packed springs
of energy often between the lines
one can admire and love these
poems, they are treasures
how to be profound, meditative and yet
quintessentially light
as we move through the darkness
of our common lives. It is not the same thing
to be a poet and to carry what it is
a poet carries, and has the courage
to press forward, as one must.

SHADES

They who have been our drinking companions
move away from us
into history
at least for a time
we too will fade
perhaps we already turn to shades of grey
we are not King Lear belting at the storm
but who will write the blood for us?
if life, as they say, is brutal and short
so be it, if unfair
the undeserving stagger on
the young, in all their promise
stop, are stopped, become symbols
prop up their own effigies
glistening in the rain.

THE DANCER

She was dancing
light-footed and lace-dressed
rising nimbly and adroitly
and with such smiling
free you would say of turmoil
and we were left dragging
heavy as we watched her
unassailable and untouched
detached from all our care

MEDITATION AT A CROSSROAD

Oh no, the impossible thought at intersections –
the words turned sour, or thought not turned at all
the cat upon the window ledge, the paper:
old things that tell us what we will not tell…
she, for it was she, invincible I'd thought
and this, inevitable, she had no meeting to recall –
we walked down many streets, some in the cold
we turned about and ran, coldly, for the time:
poets were reading in the smaller halls –
we sat where we could talk and dine.

And there is nothing I can say will make it right
the turning, the respect, the covenant
and then the confidence to say – to talk
of people on a list who seem to choose
this other path, but slowly, in an angular way
exhausted after many steps, and then declare
that is enough, we've done our duty now.

We note how bending in the stream
makes fresh wood tender – fit to form a hull
or ribbing, and we also soften thus.

PORTRAIT OF A PASSENGER

Throughout the long journey he seldom spoke
he would nod and scratch his head
look blankly through the train's window
nothing seemed to register in the present.
He was carrying, we thought, past burdens
or was it a presentiment of future eventuality?
We did not place these officers in charge:
benevolence is a mask like a child's sweet
tickets are only needed when you alight –
he listened, you could tell, not to chatter
but to the clink and rumbling, the unstable
wheels on wheels as they seemed to speak
like a kinder game, or hidden strategy –
silver edges and glinting, the old ways
forever gone, and the unrecoverable deeds
of simple doings across the counter or deck
the way he would weigh things justly
and look in each eye for a touch of respect
which in turn he gave, politely, to each one.

HENRY THE PUPPET

Was a puppet Henry
papier mâché
with a hooked nose
finger puppet in a smock
I made him
and I said now children
tell Henry all
see how he can nod
and twist his head
you can see
how he approves
and he is funny
in turn he thinks you funny
in your desire
and your despair
the way pain flowed
sometimes in your family
but you must not tell
well only to Henry
this kind of doll you
cannot cuddle well

TRIBAL RITUALS

I am hearing their voices
singing on the street
shouting to each other wildly
but we do not understand

They are another generation
breaking open another life
into something wild and frustrated
what's projected was not given

Gave them the echoes of sexuality
the maleness on top of the roof
the throbbing car and its scream
the essence of destructive wheeling

We are not of one kind you and I
our tribes have been vanquished
and the hunter who stands on the hill
is of one kind, and not another

Weapons and celebration
food and fire, by the charred light
we do these things and move out
because there is only red dust.

GOING AND COMING

Going away is easy to think about
or even plan
but it's the coming back
now while the whole world
the so-called civilized world
is drifting to suicide
why should we make sacrifices to live
they say
and surely the coffins might float
on any flood
falling or shooting or walking on water.
We think perhaps of John Henry or Ernest
and all their dying fathers
who fought before them –
heat rose as heat always does
and we were unstable when we sat to rest
thinking of going away
and how any arrival has its stress –
also any plan for coming back.

HEARING IT NOT ON THE RADIO

He is hearing it, not on the radio
and it has its rhythm:
whistle bang and fanfare, and come
back in the morning.
O come my love and answer me,
and come to me at the dairy
with a pocketful of rye;
say good it's been
what you carry,
will you carry, as well
wonder why.
The great shunting newest boat
not tall or great but solid
haul away haul away as they must
they sing a song of past deaths
and their tragedies
not being what we were
or said we were.
Song of reputation
digging did ya?
in the field and news
mix the sad as noted for
the first, the hoot, and how to stop –
I cannot hear, I cannot say.
I beauty dance.
I know this walk,
I know this step – but
none comes home   !

THE SONG OF THE FALLEN SOLDIER

I see my darling
walk with the crows
and trailing flowers
as her hand hangs down
her eyes are gleaming
and she stares at skin
a score of hazy moons
rise from her heart
she moves on slowly
our love is gone
she does not forget
how she pleaded with me
I should not go.

WE HEAR THEIR VOICES

We can still hear their voices
in earnest confrontation
making sisterhood by words of confidence
and disagreement –
what you do not tell...

And the time goes by, stolen by pirates
and menfolk
with their great dreams
and shackles for the prisoner
and all the next day promises
which they need not fulfil.

If I leave the keys in the car with you
and you keep it in the old grey shed
with the crushed cartons,
then in an emergency you have transport
if you can get it started
but he will want something flash and shiny
paid out of the accumulation
the inheritance of our patient years.

And the way computer pictures
tell lies and aspirations
we will gather to us
all our witty friends
and they will share in our fear
[...]

at the cookout with a gas barbecue
the salads, the dips, the relish
the range of marinated eats
all as provender and summer plenty.

Children playing ball in the street
abuse our ears as they disfigure Sunday
and the cars in the driveway
are moved to a safe distance.

Walk then with us, through the ailing
to the stores and bank machines
while the sky wears white whiskers
and its light dazzles the ornate of our glasses.

We can still hear their voices
confident with confidences
& I am waiting for ground transportation
the last moments of check-in.

I am leaving what I lost
on the deck there are gentle conversations –
the argot of presentation
& the language of the gods.

OLD PRINTS

We search for pictures somewhere in the box
perhaps they're dog-eared, but a trace
if we could find it, of what was –
but is no more, as Randolph would have said:
nothing can remain: even this day in the dark
will never come again, and what we have
a bird, a suitcase, written page
is just a trace, memento, relic that we know
decipher, what might make us choke a little
heading out, believing in a touch we had
where memory dared awhile with a tearful eye.

VANISHED YEARS

If you should remember yourself when young
bent to the broom or belt like Cinderella
the curses of parental derision, and the loss of hope
that one may grow eventually, as strong as that...

I have nothing for you, no great gift
and I think of the years which have vanished as they do
and how we may negotiate our time
and climb the bushy limbs, and as we check
music perhaps, and fleeting things, the ever joy
tell me the story, tell it straight or no
the forget-me-nots in the garden
the essential bloom in these cold buds
and under this cold sky
the bay forever murky with its tide
we come to this, make port
and then we try to understand.

This was your time, your age
the configuration of the wish.

THE GIFT OF ROSES

I do not bring you roses; they are yours.
I do not bring you precious stones
And I have brought you sorrows and the trial
of daily love and rancour as we toil
always it seems on a road that's rising up
and where the view's obscured, but where we hope.

I'll bring them home, the flowers and the bees
the garden implements, the place we almost made.
And it was open to our coming
we fell, you'd say, like tumble dolls
to rock, and yet to make a cheerful sway.

We count the numbers, all these awards
we math them, with a cloth
for cleaning, and a vacuum for dust and flies,
and how we see the light of this
and bless our eyes!

Not bells, for we don't have them:
not roses, nor chocolate. Then
what sweet may we aspire to –
it's nothing we could eat!

I cannot give you roses; they are yours
I have no bag of gold
[...]

we have so many books no room for more
and chocolate is set aside I think today.

You do not wear a feathered hat or cloak
the house is full of little generous gifts
so then perhaps a word or two
but you will think it's just a jest:
well nothing then, except my constant love.

It's all the things you cannot see of self
you lack a mirror which can show your worth
and no words that I write can get it all:
two eyes, a nose, a mouth a chin we know
and yes, a tongue for saying what you think
faster than writing, dry and sharp as ink.

You took it from me, patient as a test
of all the ones who love us, seeming best.

A THOUSAND MIRRORS CANNOT SHOW YOUR SOUL

A thousand mirrors cannot show your soul

If all the years are mirrors then the soul
is cast about in fragments of refraction
and the story they will tell is webbed and crossed
and what we think we know is only what we lost.

You, as we come to know you, are the song
of many singers, deed of many deeds
the inspiration of our time, the way we hope
now it's what we'd be if we could say!

Each fragment of each mirror and each touch
the pattern of a million points of light
These were the times we crossed with other lives
and felt the hands, and passed to this delight.

The pen is lonely, lost without a theme
riven by mystic forces and the breeze
I hear you, but I'm caught as you can say
here nothing comes, and nothing stays away.

I WOULD GIVE YOU

I would give you a myriad bright illuminations
like the sky when the polluted cities fade
or like the mind when brought to contemplate our lives
in all this glimmer of majestic tapestry.

These are because I've nothing left to give
a thousand heartfelt dreams and wishes blend
but nothing you can touch, and even as a rose
has interlocking petals yet is furled within its heart

I think how interleaved our pleasures and rewards.
I could send an empty page and let you sail
in contemplation, conjure paths and deeds
but now I scar it with my scribbled words –
and hope that pens can conjure as they write –
words then, mere words, that wish all hope I can
and wonders, the many years you've given me
of greatest love, and again it is: with love!

DISTANCE

A million miles from nothing
and you feel it, even if untrue
tonight a full moon bursting in the trees
and the death watch as they called it
another time, but a man in an induced coma
breathes still though tubes
they do not let him go
not yet: this time the tests are done
and they wait cautiously
with all the precision of knowing
after twenty years
when nothing can be done.

IN THIS AUTUMN LIGHT

large yellow or tangerine
small yellow or gold
in the autumn light
then they dance a little
with no consistent breeze
we have recalled past lives
according to tradition
and the way this mountain
distils for us its radiance
and the distant smoke
of many fires   .

WORLD TRAVEL

the whirr of time
on great turbines
followed by good landings
and bad
and the necessary imperious
security who check
and confiscate
and look you in the eyes
a bad photograph
is what they know you by
computers interlink
to identify you
all the fine details
of travel on another day.
It knows you –
it remembers you –
your history is
not written in the stars
but electronic data bases
eventually, after faces
and fingerprints
the DNA, and small traces
of ancestry analysed:
it seems a thousand years.

COASTAL VISTA

The bells all clang about the town
the neighbours come in throngs
the fireworks crash, the whistles blow
the air is full of songs

But you have left the southern base
you've moved to ice and rock
you climb the track above the sea
your mind is taking stock

Here was the love that you have left
the dark hair and sad eyes
the soft brown skin and slender limbs
the gentle bows and sighs

You test the mettle of your heart
by teeth at the jagged edge
you know how pain is shaped to carve
the images of mind and ledge

Taught by this landscape running strong
the chill winds from the sound
you'll drink a hot glass as you think
what magic you have found.

IT'S HELD IN BLOOD

In a state of savage rebellion
we turn back
to voices we have heard without despair
and as the tumbrels rolled in other times
we watch the trucks bump on
taking the words away.

What then, with no surrender possible
of heart or mind
and never channelled by the social need
we walk the narrow alleys of this time
alone we think, and with no end in sight.

There must be, for the lack of other name
some eloquence, and then its beauty:
like the chair nobody sees
when no one looks
but which persists as icon of the space
where some will post in time the mark
and waste things gone awry.

The boy on the beach
finds driftwood, eaten by the sand
and what remains is beautiful and fine
but it would glow in fire
not stand upon the mantle.
[...]

This was a thing of hope against the night
you see the enemies of man are only men
and what they are, these now
not of the machine
but yet a greedy thing we cannot understand.

So make the change...fill days with calculation
what is the reward the figures bring?
We turn about and turn about.

Books that are held in repositories
do not decay in usage:
the rains will come
but never wash the simple print away.

We see in this the goal –
there is no prize: we seek no grant
and no one pays for words like this to sell:
the time was held in blood.

That clock – I cannot turn it back
we cannot find the hands
here digitized and foul.

We stand
as always we have stood
alone
and in this standing
come to be like stones.

THE GRANITE STAIRWAY

The granite stairway winds into the sea
as if some god or hero made it
we know it was an ancient time
when there was magic power in limbs
and where we thought of slings to throw
or the trusted metal in a blade
and dreamt of beaten armour or chain-mail
making us invulnerable:
here every hero was defined
by details of his hair, his face
and the wonderful icons of the heraldry
stuff of children's tales – or old men's –
dreaming by the evening fire & cooking pots
a time when we would conquer things
and risk at play the things we won:
oh I was distracted when I talked of this
it was the noise of something military
beyond horizons, rattling in our sleep
as we had always talked of myths –
or like Rip Van Winkle and the great Dutch games...
the noise is there beyond the brink of history
and it is like a tide in which men drown
mired in their dreams and in their uniforms:
they are the swallows of the spring
which promises but does not dare return.

THE PATH OF BLOOD

It seemed they were skating on blood
the red surfaces glowed like evening
the blackened ridges humped so like a beast
and the glistening trees gave back the glimmer light.

It was conscience took them, and this accoutrement
into the flat dusk, to the task, preordained
but hardly understood. There was a goal
but hardly an estimate of the detail.

It was known that they crossed the precipice
edgily, in a landscape as still as a skittle
but there were no maps or intelligence
to tell of the destruction and its buckled hopes

one step or another, one slip, and the glide
the yellow cordage taut like an instrument
their hearts also, paradoxically, afloat
as it seemed to be held and yet quicken.

And there was this recognition, there was death
and many deaths before, and to come
when you cross over into this venture, no truck
and little prospect of returning in triumph.

It was done, not for splendour, but for faith:
in the skills, the routine, the recovery plan
pledged then, forbidden
but ordered like this -- to be so.

OUR LADY'S LAKE: WEXFORD

In the wind off the lake I heard no music
the white swans buckled and inverted to feed
like blocks of foam on crumpled canal-paths
and small ducks hovered gently at the edge.

It has been made a place of Christian pilgrimage
the well of the Virgin, though unsafe to drink
choked with soiled wrappers and old cartons
all tossed in disfigurement.

                        Why this procession?
Ghosts have passed by on their way to eternity
the saints return and engage in lay devotions
but we do not feel or heed their sad display.

CASTLETOWN CARNE

All those wishings by which we displace us
throw caution to the four winds:
he stood on this spot and was filled
with disquiet, heard the rumbling of caves
the hurrooing of voices in chorus or lament.

What was given was given freely, so they said
but was it for rent only? Was it a sharing?
that you should aid in future survival
and prosperity. We store things and provender;
at the table there will be much nodding and prayer.

Let us build, said he, let us build strongly
against the elements, and whatever may come
insurrection, invasion, the traducing of law
for the cords and staves intersect as a plan
and of this we have insight, and a treaty.

There is space for us and our longing – askew
and you may tell the story your northern way
if you wish, but we have our own law:
we move these rocks to make fortifications
we have our understanding and our grip.

In a statement of power – of belonging
take other men in our hands, and our hearts.

THE OLD BALLAD

Oh the dawn is breaking, my heart is breaking too
as the old song recalls, in the time of jail
and the mournful wail of stones and sighs:
there was that turning off, and turning away
to be killed by soldiers, or by shame.

Now the sad family partings, the storm,
the crossing of the sea to the port of Liverpool
I dream I swayed in the day's cloth
a desolate journey, locked below
the hunger and the values, as things go.

It was limitation, and the bonding of the soul
that would sing or play, and drink a little
outward forever, pledging to return
with gold dust in our shoes, in success –
we hear church bells – lost when our towers fell.

READING THE GRAVES

As we climb they chime
the clocks in the old church
by painted green post-boxes
and long grass
to cover all the dead names
and of course their dates
of birth and dying
pray for the soul of him or her
whose earthly remains are laid
here where a thousand years
seem little tribute
to the daily harvesting and toil
of beast and men and maid.

SOMETHING OF A BALLAD

If we could leave them as we went by
where fresh fish and mussels was the cry
we'd know how the present days ate up the past
how flowers were fallen; and what we had lost.

Oh Molly, we'd cry, you sang out your wares
And we sang them too as we sat by the stairs
but your song now is shouted by drunkards and all
who sing without music, but surely can bawl.

What we have of our time is what we can spend
on tourists and travellers, all to this end
of making a budget, the crowds to attract
and telling dishonestly tales we can act.

I'll say that I came from the foot of the mountain
I'll rise to the top in a bus that is certain
we'll see with a telescope the place where they fought
and forget all the poems they're telling for nought.

But bark like a soldier, and shout like the preacher
Look back on the days of our Christmas and Easter –
you won't hear much language here, only the patter
of beggars and cadgers who'll say it don't matter.

EXEQUY

The noughts and crosses in the graveyard
ruined now and dangerous, the church roof gone
because of taxes and a forlorn state
the sun burning haloes and broken crucifixes
where we know the unnamed are buried
the mortal remains they say, pray out of kindness
not that as a ghost or uneasy spirit to remain
but we feel them, almost hear them, the voices
hanging in the air, throughout our time
and this we did or built on our journey
one step on the road, & one step from the quay.

THE EMIGRANT HERO

You want the positive the hero
venturing as ventures come, like gold

but the other story tells how he
driven from his home in famine

ran from this coast to another
sailed at last to what he might become

failed there but left a name
something of a story, fabricated

but with a hint of talk, or myth...
how he aspired and climbed

before we tumbled into this, the ash
of many smudged days

trades that were obliterated
no one coming later could discern

which path or ladder, the ticket
faint scribbling on a copied map.

He was not, he could tell them, ever rich.

FOR DROWNED CREWMEN

what smells driven up in the sea wind
stirred for the cragged cliffs and the birds
the great carry of these stewed waters
where the drowned crewmen will not return
it is the going down and the breaking
where to be swamped and tackle tangled
we cry out to God and His Lady, and they hear
but the way it is caught up with the grey sky
and the heavenward storm-birds which rise
they will not hear the singing more
or the shouts and cries of loved ones in lament
yet the solemn procession will stir as we pass
and we'll tell our prayers slowly like a chant.

HISTORY REPEATS

Let history repeat, slowly, but suddenly
like a bad meal, regurgitate itself
you do not know which way to move the piece
you do not know the judges, how they swim
the publication of the word or sentence now
the ebbing tide and fatal tidal marks.
Oh Martin, do you hear again the rock
and do you see the bell or light for shore
and history, you know, will tell as ballads do
some tale, some tragedy, or some false hope
parting with good tidings, and the sun as fair
the way the elements bring on their own cantata
the arms of those who signal from the air –
and the silence of their message is not lost.
Go then, for we are waiting as before
and history repeats – like pieces on the shore.
Turn back from here, they'd say, and then again
you don't belong, for no one comes this way.

EMIGRANT ANCESTOR

Given what is never known
we wonder about his going
did he flee, or did he adventure?
did he repudiate the land of his birth?
and was there anger between the kin
or contrary then, did he go at his family's request
to make some kind of a start –
or for the health of his drear self
and a wounded heart?

A QUESTION OR TWO

We have them loitering here, over coffee
and asking a question or two, tentatively
before the snap of deeper words
for they have returned to pry into things
we have chosen to forget, and they construct
stories of greatness and endearment, heroics,
who faced persecution for the Faith
or chose to bury what they could not have:
this was the pot of gold, the rainbow
in all its stripes, and the way they suffered.

Now the returnees come and seek some heritage
according to the martyrdom which they escaped.
There are papers hidden here as Granny says
stories which should not be told, papers which reveal
details of secret plotting & dangerous events.

Do they think for a moment we were always free?
It is not history to sell, but it is a past
where worried souls shut in confessed
and tried to find a kind of kinship
tried to wrap stuff in a blanket thus and pray
discovery at last, that only in a forlorn faith
they'd turned their prayers to Mother of us all
and begged for kindness in their heavy grief.

DREAMING ON MY LAND

I fill my pipe and stand before the lake
meditate on land, on rent, the law
and what some men call Faith – allegiance
and who is loyal to whatever gang.
Ghosts there are, and fairies, in their dreams:
the sword of steel, the newly fashioned pike.
All they ask of me is that I hold.
But what is it I hold, this piece of land
these furrowed tracks which boil inside my head
telling the stories of the inland roads
too narrow for a cart, trodden by our feet
I pass the flax and think of how the girls
with coarsened fingers worked at spinning here
of sheep and cows, and how this herd is mine
the rent I ask for it, the land is safe
I pay my tax, my tithe, my preservation
cart grain to granary, hops to trading hours
and to myself I sing a forward song
with never grief, and pride for pushing on.

THE BARQUENTINE

While the wind is conjuring up the barquentine
making a picture of rigging and the fore and aft
jolly tales of romance on the sea
hear what the songs of Wexford tell
of fisherfolk and lifeboats and the trade
standing off or trying, and the way the storm
relentless hits the rocks, and how its jaws
will answer prayers with death, screams
with shattered windows, and hail like shot.

We tell the tales of wild November
or a darkened light in drear December
how hope is grim and is a kind of folly
to trust in faith and prayer as to the wind
with nothing but the captain's nose to then foretell
which way the rain or storm may come
and how the lifeboat crews are put at risk
where knowing seas is staying safe at home
in weather such as this grave season's time.

Oh we may pray and pay for prayers like this
and rig a bell to sound its message clear
carve on the tombstone links of broken chain
and anchors more as symbol than as sure.
We led them, stood with terror at the cliff
and watched in dread as round each point
each vessel made its narrow presence felt.

THE WEXFORD THREE

Three men, three brothers in a fragile cot
small boat that is, flat bottomed
precarious in any sea, brave Wexford boys
went out to rescue, in impossible odds
the crew of a trapped ship, at Carnsore Point...
well they died, the crew died, & the sea arose
as it does near Tuscar Rock and lights.
So all were drowned as the story goes
as it always goes in ballad and in tale.

Why do they tell it? We predict this end.
We foretell this fate, we know they are heroes
and they cry to Mary as they charge the sea:
Our Lady of the placid lake and isle
looks on, benevolent and forlorn, to pray
while we who come as pilgrims pass the shrine
and as we pray, in our despairing thought, that we
heroic too, may live, and with her help
still brave the daily seas off this sad point.

OF THE CROPPY

The birds all sang from tree to tree
and the song they sang was Ireland free
they say that song was full of joy
but the tale they told was the croppy boy.

Oh the croppy boy has long been dead
He had the name for his shaven head
He was tried for treason and was hanged so high
and the song we sing is to make us cry.

These stars have come to this solemn place
of the loss of love and the grave disgrace
But it contradicts what we'd say as he bled
giving different reasons the boy is dead.

He was not as they'd say the minstrel boy
but a lad with a yearning his youth to display
he had no person to hate or like
but he joined with the rebels and carried a pike.

The general was fat, the general was tall
they shortened his name to old Cornwall
the singers who blamed him knew this in their song
he hated that shame which did not right wrong.

But Croppy was lost, not to military spite
nor sergeant as priest, nor confession contrite
nor sentence so passed, but a subterfuge trick
no blame that was laid for his being a Mick.
[...]

The boy who was hanged no traitor was he
but a cousin betrayed him to get him a fee
and his brother stood by as they took him away
and his father denies him, or his family betray.

We say it is family, and family is blood
and down through the ages, we all understood
we're part of each other, we come from a line
where loving was honour and honour was fine.

But he mounted the scaffold and could not deny
he'd fought for his country, and he would not lie
they took him and tried him, possessed all the land
like proverbs all tell of a bird in the hand.

THREE SAILORS

A Mahon, a Murphy, a Cavanagh
the lonely three, lost, never returned
& we dream they were swept out
picked up, carried away on sail
crew that might return some day
where we have mourned.

Oh but he would not write, she said
he could not. He could play
and climb or throw, but not with a pen
nor all that paper stuff –
he did not read, and what we found
was broken timber in the tide
and lives that lived to sail.

Forgotten men are not forgotten here
the date of sailing, weather calm
favourable wind, and then the gale
swept up it seemed from a hurricane
the ocean is untaught untied upturned:
it does not play by rules.

And in our pagan hearts perhaps
we think the gods could intervene
but for our saints we know that prayer
leads us to sadness and the chant:
the Lady's will should bring them home
and bless them with her caring hands.

LAMENT

No one plays these tunes
and no one sings them slow
as they should be

in a key which is wrong or uncertain
in the dirge of heartfelt grief...
they're relieved by thirst grasping a little

or prayer for the dead, the lost
the unexplained
except that it is thus

it is what we think we own
these passages to grief
and things unspoken

because though the eyes are eloquent
throat rises and the sounds
gurgle a little but the words

never will they come
except to say perhaps
on the next day morning

the sky and its horizons still are there
and we can think perhaps
it will calm down itself in some short while.

A SECTARIAN STRUGGLE

the bloodstains on the flat stones
like maps or gruesome child art
set out the martyrdom as it's called
traces of the butchery, or indeed
the curse of one killer and recrimination.

we are left with maps and diagrams
each one step closer to elimination
we move toward the cataclysm as foreseen
and there are clouds of black smoke rising
in a heaven which tries to sparkle blue

but here the draughty robes and masks
leave only the assurance that a threatening voice
speaks loudest, and the crowds which gather
do not know where the game is to be played
or the next step in this dire test unfold.

POETS OF THE ASCENDANCY

They say that many Irish poets were of the ascendancy —
Protestant, that is, like William Yeats
but associated with Catholic writers who joined them
by conversion perhaps, or simply by being rich.

You can hide behind your cousin if you will
and that is why the woman, who could not vote
would yet control the land, or birthright of the cross
walking this way or that, and with a text
or with repeated prayers and pilgrimage.

Then do we walk in procession, or do we stand?
Do we shout the songs or kneel and pray?
Do we banish from our minds the faults of men?
Forget these things and wrestle with muses
or the vigorous sports they played to keep us still!

BALLAD OF CRUSADES AND CHASTITY

What will you mark? What will you say?
As the dirty stones blanch white.
Here was the abbey pledged to our God
and the loss of the lovers at night.

O Alex, my dear, O marching back home
from Christendom now you are come
but the story you hear will tear your soul down
and the tears will be painful as blood.

You went to the wars, and you kept all your faith
to God and our Master of Rolls
You rode many miles, and fought many times
your heart was not frozen with hate.

I told you then, yes I told you, my boy
That girl's not the right one for you
For I am your mother, and I am so proud
and a fortune I'm saving for you.

Riding high and trotting low
Singing the song of the spurs
Crying death to the Saracen
and the blood of the swinging arm!

But he came home and she was gone:
she thought her crusader was slain
and took all the vows of a cloistered nun
so he built him an abbey and walled it with stone.

AFTERMATH

Warriors and champions all
made peace with the slain
that they might live in renown
do battle again
and with the charm
of magic, pure water, and the feast
with venison and great music
songs they sang again.

Oh we have sung old battles
and willing daughters
castles and celebration
that here there comes each father
seeking truce from heroes
engendered love in triumph
the magic spells can teach
forever in their arms.

IN THE WHISKEY BAR

Opening time in the bar
they say it is always there
for one brand or another
the whiskey tourists drink
the other for those who know
Dublin has its pubs
and its great breweries
industry and the collective interest
of tradition – music
the inevitable noise
when a wistful man with arms crossed
gazes at the ceiling
reflects on pottery, pie-plate, golf
television intercedes with people's dreams
and we trek home now
line after line of colourful busses
things we recall when we awake.
It is a long time till morning.
And we tried the Power's:
they say it's like any other
to the non-connoisseur.

WE TRAVEL ON

Past all the crises and accidents
the decisions we took without regret
tremulous journeys to the unforeseen
and the great cliffs over the dark ocean

you see the lights round corners in the night
so which shall we say is safer: speedy day
or the stark glare of a touring light – on black?

eventually we all return or say, come back
some other way, on a tedious country track
and we live with it, sometimes suppressed.

One day is not the same as another: the season
shakes its way through a global calendar
and when we have nothing to reveal we ask
what kind of day, will it rain or shine?

We know, but it does not matter.
And the trees which toss in salutation
always the same unless they fall.

THE BAND ON PARADE

Horns of love and death
Herald the changes of our universe.
Crude this may be, but configured.
Blunt becomes essential elegance
And the twisted tubes of metal
Respond to three-fingered valves.
The lips to the lungs and cheeks
The heart to the elemental mind
And the force of the drum is matched
By soaring antiphonal passages.
Grim mouths and tightened brows
Military splendour of crowds queuing
The foot-beat controlled by fervour.
March on we say and never miss a step.
They will fly perhaps to other lands;
Pry open conflicts and the noisy fray.
The command is led to seem immortal:
All honour on display and full of puff.

AS TIME WORKS ITS WAY

I am sitting on the back steps and lying to myself.

Telling stories is a way of letting the brain relax,
so we tone things down by being the hero of our dreams
remembering the time we crossed that river in the flood
or the way the land comes back when the hidden seeds
begin to sprout.

There is an insistent smell about the fowl-yard.
It is not from fertilizer or the chooks;
damp hay begins to rot and to ferment.

I remember how stale things were left in buckets by the door;
and the way the muddy boots cleaned up when they were dry.

I am sitting on the back step waiting for the sun
and I think the mud will turn to powder by and by
scraped with the edge of a knife, a brush or an old toothbrush.

We hang things on the line and watch the shadows sway;
but there is nothing in it for us: let time still work as it does.

SIN

An angel might say
all sin is serious, even the venial –
but an archangel being close
might intercede
how can mere humans climb the ladder?
and what is, after all
this life which they called mortal
but to die
and in the grace of being loved
know this
to be loved is then to be forgiven
if you will
so all is serious
even if you sin
and if you laugh
and even if you open to a love
not carnal
but opening as the rose
to what is given
as a grace
and lifted, not with wings
but with the radiant sense
of what it is to be a child
whose parent says, I love:
for you, my child, I die
for you, my child, come back
come bless, forgive, again.

OLD COAT ON A PEG

I found the pocket empty.
What would you expect?
old clothes, some hung, some bundled
and he wore them, or I wore them, once
but even the old familiar smells are gone.
Just, instead, the mouldy smell of cloth
somewhere, sometime – a mothball
and even that too, faded to a whiff
just a touch – it is the mind palavers:
cold damp days in the football stand
the smoking compartment of the train
the bush walk by the windy bay;
time had its towers and vistas then
even in 620 film, even in black and white –
but I had hopes, on folded slips of paper
perhaps a wrapper or a ticket stub
evidence perhaps, confirming we were there.

THE SYSTEM

For Marshall McLuhan the nervous centre –
electronic and multifused –
confessed our bombardment of many tricks
with no overpass or subtle access.
I think it is so.

The successful parasite blooms
while the cards fall as they may
and accidents recall themselves
electric predictions.
I think it is so.

It was ramps I thought of –
exits and exits –
the clear green signs
over and underpasses.
We are not like that.

We fuse our cross-directions
leap or fall on parapets.
Somehow we survive
blend into a configuration.
Yet bloom as would a flower.

VOICES IN THE BAR

He could not know the last words of the song
and Rosamund or Rosalind
seemed all too fair – to him
and if confused, another word for strange
and this was true, the pedestal was here
reserved for visitors with training
and with all they'd brought from overseas
invaders of artistic inland space
where home-grown talents gathered in a bar
and drank or sang their sorrows
perhaps with melody and with a glass
but never with aplomb or great applause
reserved for those imported stars
who fell, he'd say, into this little space.

YOU WILL WAIT HERE

Spring from me – spring to me, with the call...
this is no port for trade, hardly a port.

Your living alone torments you
and takes you down...the well is dry.

I cannot guide you round the fire.
I cannot stir what you forgot.

Lassitude will drain you on the path:
the fishing fleet is gone, and who knows where.

This is no place for strangers: and picture:
the waiting for the wine – not so exotic.

They loved you once, and saw in you
the promise of a land which now is dry.

You should cling there, and build a dome
which replicates the sky.

It's easy then this masquerade
but not for a lover who betrayed.

I think you strangled what you had
and then the bones lay dried.

And greater care than this was had
if you interpret what they wrote.
[...]

You have many miles to travel and to stay
all for home this farm, and back again.

So you will go down to the sea
and watch for craft which still may come.

STAY A LITTLE

What I have lost is a dangerous thing
cast as a biscuit into the foam
in dereliction falling down
I have no direction for it – no dedication.

the clamour of gathered walkers raising hands
blots out our deliberation on this spot
and the broken clasps where linesmen worked
are scant to any who pressure and take note.

I am past medication, past introspection
the ruffled sands show ancient marks
as the writing of new and old debris
always remains as a tide's direction.

Does it swim in air? Is the pattern taken?
Do the angels swoop past the earth with wings?
Hold on. Stay steady. We are here this moment.
It is still. It is magic. It has its eternal glow.

THE FLOOD

swirling like a
damaged stream
the yellow flood
of our destination
to escape if we can
over these pathetic
hills and far away
down there in the
little village
of pain we visit
prolonged agony
submerged history
as it once was
as it once was then.

MUSEUM TOWN

We get to the point where every town
is a museum town. We have been here before.
We remember as it was – the barrels and sticks
the echo of the floorboards and some old fold
some chat, and the way Jack always said –
well I won't quote him, the score –
and we replied, similarly, as he knew.

But the books and old photos tell
more and other than our recollection.
Everything fades or is sepia; the flesh departs
the essential ribbons and woven threads
the roll of fabric, the test of provender…
we can see them, but hear no more.

And I could tell you a thing or two
but it's private and I don't want to hurt
the living or the dead, and all their kind.
But every town remains a museum town
and every town we visit is our past.

THE DOLLS

In China the dolls sit on a shelf
in red and gold to wish good luck
In Singapore they serve your tea
and bring good fortune so they say.

But here our seats and coats are rough
we say we dream; we do not think.
These things passed by: and all they know
is what was promised years ago.

THE WORM

There are two creatures, both animal:
one is that bird which carries the worm
the other is the circular black crawling worm.
The second could be free, in plants and drains
for the worm is circular and tough.
The magpie is familiar and struts
always just a distance away, in triangular paths.
I think of these as trajectories
where the mind tries to formulate
a necessary circle, necessary line
the way we come to understand
something – because there is always beyond –
rotation, restlessness, the pattern of life
which isn't much if you are eaten
except you demonstrate an elemental design
cipher for the geometric page
and then in this, the possibility
of a mathematical encounter
with the bird, who will push at it
and always seem full of knowledge
bearing this instant cipher in its beak.

STITCHES

stitches
like cartographers' diagrams
pierce
and bind

the fruitful weed
loops under soil
coveting
all nourishment

the depleted
herb
hangs
weakens a little

till in the rain
with clipping
and deft hands
the gardener

delves
draws
sutures and binds
blends well.

DON'T TAKE YOUR BAT TO TOWN

Tie him to the post, Mother
that he might not get out to wound
destroy the violent threatening men
or gang of boys outside the light
the silhouettes of shapes with kitchen implements
the scrapes and whistles of derision
he will want to break the bonds, Mother
for something less than honour
the elemental challenge of his rage
to answer all their call
and by the gas fire he feels heat
controlled by pipes and taps
and not the ancient fury of the maze;
he will wait for you to untie him, Mother
go pleasant, with bat and ball
toward the park, to wait
as if to play, but then to swing
and knock their heads and teeth
daytime in the colour of the blood
where she untied the grasp
as one or other lies at last
the earth and bloody wound to head
as we foretold it would.

WAITING FOR FATHER
Richmond 1921:

Down Charles Street the children are locked in.
They are cowed and all their savagery gone
rigid in the knowledge that frayed cuffs
do not destroy self-yearning respectability
and the way a once deep love draws them
as they wait by wire gates for a whistle
hear the rattle and shake of uneven steps
not allowing themselves to wonder, or to ask.

There will be tea with only a drop of milk
saved to go with the bought jam tarts at night
and the way the nodding shoulders give assent
of a kind to the way this street leads out
to all the lessons life can seem to teach
and the money gone, the way each coin is held
tight as you find the essential foods of love:
potatoes and bits of meat and forgotten cans
bags of broken biscuits to dip in the tea.

THAT ALMOST PERFECT POEM

Will I turn back to that learned poem?
erudite and presumptuous, the autobiographical myth
only as I might say, an example
clearly dragged out or drawn – a terrain
where I do not want to go.

And yet it is an almost perfect poem
light on the syrup, exact of definition
presumptuous a little of the very late poet's mind –
well I knew him, you did not, and wonder
just what you would make of his precinct
supposedly, as opposed to your suburb (real)
pinned down as imagined, assumed
and thus, you'd better believe it, heavily drawn
not as John Ashbery would, who'd not go there
but nationalizing us, as if an act: the dog,
the bed, the loving wife, the child.
Where did that other culture come in here
cry and blanket it, said as you roll it out?
I'll stagger then, and pee, and turn the book.
I'll save whatever part I bought or had
because a publication asked us to review.

CROSSING ON THE FERRY

I

In the ferry salon
the nostalgic photographic art
orange and beige-patterned
with rotating seats on silver stands
and white circular tables
also on silver stands
scattered in apparent random
(well you can move them)
in a flat open space
twelve of them in no array
all in this quarter of a limited deck
and the constant gentle buzz
of conversation on a Sunday afternoon
to Geelong or Queenscliff and return
checking to take photographs and eat pies or tarts
& to enjoy this space.
[...]

II

Nearby an old lady, everybody's aunt
with an old lady Australian accent and that voice!
declares into her cell phone
we sail at six o'clock
we sail at six o'clock
Sail? we shudder and heave
as she shuts off
the peninsula slides sideways
it seems – yet to seem so still
the hotels and towers swim as well
a circus merry-go-round is started
and the bubbling children
full of this – ooh and aah
they make a romp
bubble chatter raucous noises
and middle ages wave good-bye
from the windy deck
to people quite unseen
the waving continues outside
they wave it seems to shops and towers
she can't see us she says
she can't see us
and still they chatter on
we are welcomed aboard
by a clanging metallic recording
and by the old lady – a woman
with a laugh like a tin opener
ripping their space apart.
[...]

III

The ferry has its twin
they cross each other
convivially
and the flat sea
is dimpled grey
they carry the unequivocal pattern
quietly where birds congregate
like an abrasive surface
nesting on a flat rock
we know this traffic
feel it in our bones
it's changeable, yes
and unutterably the same
don't give us the ice
or hot drinks
don't give us fizz
but know all this
the tide of summer
drifting into night.

IN SOME FUTURE TIME

It is very difficult for me to write this thing
knowing that in some future time
I will be called a liar or pretender.
They'll say (well who are they?) these words
are not my own, and nominate
some other chap, well-known perhaps or not
who penned these lines
and they will plead his case.
They'll say I did not do the thing I did:
deflower maidens, balance pots of beer
ride wildly through the night
and sing love songs or folk, well they will say
he could not carry such a tune
and as to writing one, or even words
look at his clumsy style, his dreary life
it may be, they will say he has a claim
to be so many generations of a Bacon
and to a wife from Oxford if you know
well, wife of Oxford, there's a tattling joke
and even that he lived in Worcester once
and was familiar with the poets there.
They'll say he had two daughters
as he did, and there was music,
and some trade or shipping in his line.
But I must be, or so they say, a sham
pretending to be this thing
a man both driven, and yet driven out
[...]

to run from town to country
and country into town.
a charlatan who thought that words were magic
and could transform a scene
or even gain him entry to the village hall
or old museum where his part was read.
Wounded, as they said of us, but never say we're dead.
(Vulneratus non victus)[1]

---

[1] Pretenders to the authorship of Shakespeare's plays included Bacon and Oxford. Shakespeare's Stratford is in the region of Worcester. After the playwright's death his King's Players were actually paid by the town not to play in Stratford. I happen to have a Bacon ancestor, and a wife from Oxford. I did live in Worcester (USA) where there is a vibrant poetry scene. My true surname is Codd, and the (rather strange) family motto is quoted at the end of the poem. *Vulneratus non victus:* wounded not dead meat! – or: wounded not conquered.

THEY SEEMED TO BLOOM

Now there are flowers where there were none.
He read many poems which seemed to bloom
pacing deliberately and with deliberation
such a determinate – and he demanded
is it then? or must it be so? must it?
such contrasts in the mutually derivative
must it? He then thought, must it deliberate
pushing a heavy lower lip closing from
the words then, a narrative of thought
that here the echo judges, & must concern
must squiggle and probe, weigh and conclude
a verb of such intent, and locking down.
Turn now to that deliberation which seems
I'd say, like a prior sense of mind.
A serf abhors the state of what is king
and is more feather-like, more of a state;
we'd run for it, and see what buds are there
after we dead-head all the faded blooms
so that we make no flowers, but the buds;
and to the sunny rain which opens hands
and glows, responds, irradiates the air
but you will cut or pin them down
resplendent as they seem: they are, they are
just as the spring should say a bloom should be
and muse on festivals, and so we here reflect
hardy with deliberate probing to cut down.

I WAS NOT THERE

I had to confess I was not there
when they said I was
I was tying my shoelace
on the other side of the mall
and I did not confess to the action
presupposed in their conjecture
I was buying an ice cream
double-headed, in danger of its dribble
and my suit was smart as day
echoing my own young step
and the way that custom, the flow,
people by the pier
caught my eye as they were texting
and our limited conversation
was conducted in fingers
limited by the ice cream as it melted
so I cast it in a nearby bin
& wiped my hands
which remained sticky
so I went to the tap
and washed myself clean
to send and receive
as I did – but I was not
as I said, where they said I was
from their extrapolation of mixed signals –
and for the boat I missed that day.

Selected comments:

"... a strong Shakespearean influence that stretches the mind to deeper appreciations."

"the poetry is a diverse and varied tapestry on themes tailored to an individual personal expression that is stimulating, emotive and thought-provoking...like a mature bottle of wine..."

"I take great pleasure in the way the intellect and passion drives through each poem generating its imagistic sequence. "

"...both a powerful argument and plea for more meaningful communication in our increasingly electronic, dislocated world, and ultimately very moving."

"...there's a dusty dusky flavour in this
but also a strangely academic sense
which I relate to but am kind of removed from."

"the satires, and the variation in style, and the quirky Code-like humour."

"I drank from the cauldron...There is much tenderness, much cleverness, a sense of fun, exquisite grammar, punctuation and formatting. .a brilliant literary master...*tour de force.*"

"*Stage by Stage* was a tremendous pleasure to read. A beautiful book from cover to cover. "

"I have been surprised and delighted by this book...the old punch is still there in the purer vision that knows it doesn't see the emperor's clothes – except hanging in the closet."

"The musicality of the poems is beautiful...I felt that I have been missing a sound in poetry --- for the last decade - but I have found it in these poems. This book deserves a big publisher such as Norton's. Wow!"

"This book has become my morning book, poems with tea and toast."

"In a way, the poem affords meaning to sound: aural pleasure, fluidity of movement, and what I will call: visual sound, sound which is arrived at cerebrally during the course of letters and words repeatedly being viewed by the eyes when reading in silence."

"I especially like the energy of the poems, and the way in which the poet so deftly mixes lyrical impulses with edgier, more 'experimental' ones."

"He is an accomplished poet, and the collection is a pleasure."

"... the observation pieces, the experiments ... with just this degree of play among simple structures and unextravagant subject.) ...haunting in its sparseness and bleakness."

"Witty and frightening, urban and strangely rural, unified by variety."

"I love to savor these poems before I go to sleep."

Ódrerir Books

Trevor Code, *Stage by Stage.*   2009

Trevor Code, *For One Brief Instant.*   2009

Geoff Campbell, *Words in Common.*   2010

Trevor Code, *Which Way the Wind.*   2010

Trevor Code, *Configurations.*   2012

www.ingramcontent.com/pod-product-compliance
Lightning Source LLC
Chambersburg PA
CBHW050645160426
43194CB00010B/1815